My Skateboard

Written by Maoliosa Kelly

Photographs by Steve Lumb

Collins

My pads.

My helmet.

My skateboard.

My friends.

My turn.

Yes!

 Ideas for reading

Written by Alison Tyldesley MA PGCE
Education, Childhood and Inclusion Lecturer

Reading objectives:
- use phonic knowledge to decode regular words and read them aloud accurately
- read and understand simple sentences
- demonstrate understanding when talking with others about what they have read

Communication and language objectives:
- express themselves effectively, showing awareness of listeners' needs
- use past, present and future forms accurately when talking about events that have happened or are to happen in the future
- develop their own narratives and explanations by connecting ideas or events

Curriculum links: Physical development; Personal, Social and Emotional Development

High frequency words: my.

Interest words: pads, skateboard, helmet, friends, turn.

Word count: 11

Resources: two small card strips for each child.

Build a context for reading

- Look at the front cover together. Discuss what the book might be about. Read the title.

- Walk through the book, looking at the pictures. Leave pp14–15 to explore later. Discuss what happens. *This boy enjoys skateboarding.* Ask the children what they enjoy doing.

- Ask them to find the word 'my' on each page. *What sound does this word begin with?*

- Ask the children what the boy does first, next and at the end. *What does he feel like on p11 when it is his turn?*

Understand and apply reading strategies

- Read the book together from the beginning. As the children read, prompt and praise correct matching of spoken and written words particularly correct reading of the word *my*.

- Ask them to find words on the page (skateboard, helmet and pads). How did they find it? (I looked for a word beginning with 's'.)

- When you've read the book, look at pp14–15. Discuss with the children whether the skateboard jump was a new experience for the boy. *How did the boy feel before the jump? How did he feel when he had finished jumping?*

- Discuss the sequence of the book. Ask children to say in their own words what happened,' first', 'next' and 'in the end'.